BOOK WORMS

Transformations in Nature

A Seed Becomes a Pumpkin

Amy Hayes

Cavendish Square

New York

Published in 2016 by Cavendish Square Publishing, LLC
243 5th Avenue, Suite 136, New York, NY 10016

Copyright © 2016 by Cavendish Square Publishing, LLC

First Edition

Website: cavendishsq.com

This publication represents the opinions and views of the author based on his or her personal experience, knowledge, and research. The information in this book serves as a general guide only. The author and publisher have used their best efforts in preparing this book and disclaim liability rising directly or indirectly from the use and application of this book.

CPSIA Compliance Information: Batch #CW16CSQ

All websites were available and accurate when this book was sent to press.

Cataloging-in-Publication Data

Hayes, Amy.
A seed becomes a pumpkin / by Amy Hayes.
p. cm. — (Transformations in nature)
Includes index.
ISBN 978-1-5026-0816-1 (hardcover) ISBN 978-1-5026-0814-7 (paperback) ISBN 978-1-5026-0817-8 (e-book)
1. Pumpkin — Juvenile literature. I. Hayes, Amy. II. Title.
SB347.H39 2016
635'.62—d23

Editorial Director: David McNamara
Copy Editor: Rebecca Rohan
Art Director: Jeffrey Talbot
Designer: Stephanie Flecha
Senior Production Manager: Jennifer Ryder-Talbot
Production Editor: Renni Johnson
Photo Research: J8 Media

The photographs in this book are used by permission and through the courtesy of: D7INAMI7S/Shutterstock.com, Smileus/Shutterstock.com, cover; ©iStockphoto.com/Karen Sarraga, Roger Spooner/Photographer's Choice/Getty Images, 7; redmal/E+/Getty Images, 9; J Erwin Robert/ Science Source/Getty Images, 11; Irina Borsuchenko/shutterstock.com, 13; Datacraft Co Ltd/ imagenavi/Getty Images, 15; Enzo D./ Moment Open/Getty Images, 17; Denis and Yulia Pogostins/ shutterstock.com, 19; Elena Elisseeva/shutterstock.com, 20.

Printed in the United States of America

Contents

All pumpkins start as seeds.

5

Pumpkin seeds are planted in the ground.

A **shoot** grows from a pumpkin seed.

It will become a **root**.

9

A **sprout** shoots up from the ground.

11

The sun shines,
and the pumpkin plant
grows bigger.

13

A **flower** blooms.

A bee lands on the flower.

The bottom of the flower starts to grow.

17

It grows big and round.

It is turning into a pumpkin!

When it turns orange,
it has become
a pumpkin!

New Words

flower (FLOW-ur) The colorful leaves of a plant where fruit and seeds are made.

root (ROOT) Part of the plant that grows underground.

shoot (SHOOT) Part of a new plant that is just beginning to grow.

sprout (SPROWT) A shoot that comes up from the ground.

Index

About the Author

Amy Hayes lives in the beautiful city of Buffalo, New York. She has written several books for children, including *Hornets, Medusa and Pegasus, From Wax to Crayons*, and *We Need Worms!*

About BOOKWORMS

Bookworms help independent readers gain reading confidence through high-frequency words, simple sentences, and strong picture/text support. Each book explores a concept that helps children relate what they read to the world they live in.